A DIAMOND ASANTI SHORT STORY:

BRINGING JAZZ TO MALTA, HOTEL GORTINA

BY RUDY D'DUDE

ONRUSH MEDIA GROUP

This book is dedicated to all self-made entrepreneurs of the past, present and future.

Rudy D'Dude

SERIES 1

After reaching millionaire status before entering the second year of his military career as an officer, Diamond a self-assured Tuskegee Graduate, already knew he was on his way to fortune. After being honorably discharged from the United States Navy, Diamond opened the Shupavu Investments with his own money to focus on arbitrage opportunities in the stock market during the post-dot.com bubble crash. Within 4 years he has become a billionaire and has expanded his company from Shupavu Investments to Shupavu Equity. A holding company, where Diamond and his team are inquiring and investing in equity for profitability while re-investing in urban communities throughout the United States.

This is the beginning of his story, as he builds his empire.

"Mr. Asanti, we have opened our new real estate fund 4 months ago. We have invested thus far inland throughout Shreveport, however, I believe we should look at some cash flow fixed assets that have or may have the potential to brighten our company's portfolio." Spoken by Thomas "TD" Downing, sharing his thoughts during the beginning of the upper management meeting.

Diamond, inhale and exhale as he looks over the Treme and 7th Ward area from his building.

"Thomas, that is a great idea. Actually, I want to go a little bigger and exotic with our next investment...... Have any of you ever visit Malta?" Diamond asking his upper management team.

KyDouglas Barker responded with excitement, "Yes Mr. Asanti, I have been there, a real party island.... Sir."

Diamond smiled because of knowing, like KyDouglas, they are both United States Military Veteran Officers who have served their country, finishing with an honorable discharge and a lifetime of experience.

Diamond than turned to his team, "Ladies and Gentlemen, there's an island north of Africa and south of Italy that has been planted in the Mediterranean Sea. And there's a hotel on this island that I want this business to be a part of....... Hotel Gortina, a spa resort...."

"SLIEMA MALTA!" KyDouglas shouting with excitement... "Oh, sorry sir."

"KyDouglas, look like you had a vivid experience in Malta. We're all adults, why don't you share with us your experience there in a professional business manner, of course." Diamond said as he chuckles from KyDouglas reaction of excitement.

As KyDouglas stood up and cleared his throat, "Ladies and Gentlemen, we all know that Shupavu is the up and rising holding company that is grabbing the attention of investment firms, begging us to go public...... Malta is not just an exotic investment, this is an opportunity to show Wall Street that we are for real. Meaning, this is the up and coming premier African, European and Middle Eastern young professional relax destination, an unknown tourist hotspot...... as well as those wealthy United Kingdom parents who send their spoil early-20s children to go party for the summer just because they did not get kicked out of college. Over 1 million tourists visit per year and growing. That is almost tripling the local residents..... With all that being said, Hotel Gortina Spa Resort is about close to the middle of all action as Canal is to the French Quarters. However, I think we should grab two or more hotels instead of one."

"Thank you, KyDouglas, why 2 or more?" Ida Walker asked

"Allow me to answer that for you, KB!" Phylicia Walker eager to answer her twin sister Ida's question.

Diamond smiled as he watched his team get engulfed into a harmony of brainstorming and strategizing.

"That's what I like to see in my team, let the imagination and ideas flow." Diamond instructed

"Colleagues, as much as we try to stay off the mainstream spotlight, if we only buy one, that will bring attention to every other billion dollars holding company around the world….." Phylicia spoke

"Exactly!" KyDouglas passionately shouted

"Ummskmm" Phylicia clears her throat.

"…… Our colleague KB is suggesting that we will need to get as much equity in as many hotels or real estate as we can, so we can be at the beginning, and ride the market price as it rises."

 Phylicia presented.

"Thank you, Ms. Phylicia….. Thomas, what is the balance of the real estate fund?" Diamond asked

"Mr. Asanti, it is still over $2.7billion," Thomas responded.

"Alright, team, we are going to do 2% of the fund to invest in commercial real estate throughout Malta. I want to know all the potential 3 and 4-star hotels that can become 4 and 5 stars. Also, we need to plan a series of entertainment attraction to keep Malta on tourist minds. Have your staff to have the research done for me by close of business on tomorrow." Diamond spoke

"Yes sir!" as the team break from the meeting.

Diamond than walked toward the window to look at his view over the neighborhoods he has grown up in during the summers with his parents. Yet, smiling, enjoying the feel of the thrill as he embarks into his first international venture.

2 hours before the closing of the stock market, Mr. Diamond is on the phone talking with his lead stock trader Raymond Alexander, advising, yet, ordering him to buy European Government Bonds and a large block of Diageo's stock after it had dipped for the third straight week.

"Raymond, I respect your intellect, but right now I can care less, purchase it!" Diamond in a still yet demanding tone of voice.

While on the phone, Diamond hears a knock at his door.

"Mr. Asanti, it is Thomas, I have the Malta report." Thomas spoke

"Spider, go handle that, you'll understand later. And go learn some Guizhou language and be ready to travel to China." Diamond referring to his childhood friend's nickname Raymond "Spider" Alexander.

Diamond hangs up the phone, and shouted: "Come in Tom"......... "Mr. TD, what do you have for me?"

"Mr. Asanti, Malta and Hotel Gortina is a great idea. The resort is less than 8 miles from the airport, however, this will be at our leverage, as well as no inside entertainment due to the capacity issues. We can capitalize on all this. They do not offer an airport shuttle to the hotel, nor do they have consistent a lineup of entertainers that can perform in their entertainment ballroom. Right now, they are holding on by the thread of their brand and the 5 stars. The building and land combined are worth 133.6 million pounds. The shares of equity are split up in 2 ways, 25% to the government and 75% (100% of the real estate) privately owned by a British company by the name of "Hawkin, Jesus, and Company (HJC)" Thomas presented.

Diamond stood there as if he has 4 thoughts in his head all at one time. Then he stood up from his desk and walked toward the window.

Diamond mumbled "Hawkin, Jesus & Company?"....at a lower tone, "Ok, TD, first call Phylicia Walker and tell her to buy up a large sum of land and property in Jamestown, Virginia and surrounding areas within 20 miles. Up to $30 Million of the R.E. fund. And tell Mr. KyDouglas Barker and Ms. Ida Walker to be ready for a business conference with the HJC..... TD, how Amir James Clothing doing since the merger?"

"Great sir!.... Matter of fact, from our bi-weekly report, their sales revenue is up by 8 percent. The campaign for I Am American Too is paying off." Thomas

"Yes, let's keep them relevant, especially in the community. Matter of fact, tell the research team to find zone areas in Atlanta between Bankhead and College Town.... Let's start an annual jazz and soul festival, use Amir James as one of the sponsors so the community knows we're real. Let's do one as well." Diamond

"Where? Around city park or M.L.K?" Thomas

"No, between Treme and the 7th Ward." Diamond

After numerous conversations back and forth with hotel's executives and lawyers, Diamond assembled his team which consists of Ms. Kendra B Well, Ida Walker, KyDouglas Barker and the retained lawyer for the trip to Malta.

As they all congregated at Louis Armstrong Airport and being seated in their reserved first-class seats, Diamond turned around and reminded them "Things go as planned, we will be in the company's jet next time we fly."

Diamond express that as a reason of motivation as they embark to Malta to meet with the negotiation team of HJC.

As they transferred planes at London's Heathbrow Airport to board Air Malta with an hour and a half wait, Diamond decided to walk around to find another bar and have a drink or two while the team eat at a different restaurant and work on their negotiation strategy. As he walked toward the bar, he quickly notices a beautiful, curvy-toned brunette woman already seated, ordering her drink.

Without any hesitation, Diamond walked up to her, and said: "Pardon me, your man would not be upset if I sat next to you, would he?"

She looked with a smirk on her face as if she didn't understand what he was saying. Diamond quickly reverted to his broken French, "Belle dame, puis-je m'asseoir a cote de vous?"

She laughed out loud as the bartender brings her Raspberry Martini and spoke, "Please halt before you say something horrible in whatever other languages you try to speak to me."

Diamond gave her a smiled, and she, in her strong British accent, "Have a seat dear. I am not pushing time at this moment."

Diamond sat down and shook her hand.

"My name is Naomi and yours?" Naomi asked

"I am Diamond, and what a pleasure it is to meet you after an almost 9 hours flight," Diamond responded

"Yes, you seem to be great company, and you are flying from the America I am assuming?" Naomi

"Yes, I am, New Orleans matter of fact. And you're from?" Diamond with a smile.

"I live here now in London with my mother who also lives here as well." Naomi

"I understand…." Diamond

Before Diamond could get the 3rd word out of his mouth, Naomi shouted "Oh my God! I forgot, my boyfriend, will be here soon."

Diamond, with a disappointing facial expression, smirked, began to leave before he had ordered his drink. As he begins to walk away, Naomi laughed out loud.
"I am joking with you!" Naomi snickered….. "Oh darling, your facial expression was so puppy sad"…. As she takes the last sip of her martini, she shouted: "Oh, bartender?!"

Diamond sat back down with a humble grin on his face as the bartender walks toward them.

"I'll have another one this time with Grey Goose Vodka instead of the vodka you have used on the last mix," Naomi ordered

"Raspberry martini with Grey Goose Vodka, and for you sir?" the bartender asked

"I'll have a double shot of Courvoisier Cognac," Diamond responded as he sat down and looked Naomi directly with a smile.

"Raspberry martini with Grey Goose Vodka, and Courvoisier Cognac, double shot." Bartender repeating their order.

Naomi smiles back at Diamond.

"Very funny, very funny…. It's ok, I like a woman with a sense of humor, I believe it is sexy because that means she has an imagination." Diamond

The bartender brings them their drinks.

"Auuuh darling you were looking very sad and cute at the same time." Naomi laughs…. "I am only on my second drink and I am already having a blast WITH YOU. "
Diamonds laugh with her as well.

"Well, here is to being merry and enjoying life." Diamond spoked

"Cheers" Naomi responded

After taking their sip, Diamond asked, "So where is a lovely lady like you going?"

"My my my, aren't we a bit noisy." Naomi

"No, not at all, I thought we were on friendly grounds since you have broken the ice with your joke." Diamond

"We are, I am just pulling your leg again, and I am enjoying looking at your lips." Naomi

"Naomi, you're too funny" Diamond

"You have no idea how much fun I can be…. But I am on my way to an island called Malta on business. And you? What brings you on this side of the world?" Naomi

Diamond took a sip of his Courvoisier, looked Naomi directly in her eyes with a weighty facial expression, and responded, "I am an international stripper and adult actor, my stage name is the number 5, abbreviation for feet "ft" and the plus symbol all together it says "5ft+".

Naomi cracked a smile but was holding her laughter within as she awaited for Diamond to finish sipping his drink anc continue the theatrical jest.

"Yes, this is my 2nd Euro Tour, I am calling it, Chocolate Sprinkles," Diamond said before cracking a smile followed by a burst of laughter.

"I almost fell for that, you are too wicked and naughty to be coming up with such a joke" Naomi as she continued snickering.

Diamond slightly leaned forward, toward Naomi with a smile and responded "Oh, well you have no idea how much wicked and naughty I can be…. But I am an investor and visiting Malta as well." … in his mid-low voice tone.

The thought of Diamond being the Diamond Asanti of Shupavu Equity just popped into Naomi's head as she turns up the volume of questions.

"Really! Pleasant surprise Mr. Diamond Asanti!?! I wasn't expecting to see you here, more of greeting you at the airstrip as you fly in on your jet….." Naomi

"My jet? My jet is being…." Diamond before being interrupted by Naomi

"Darling, I was told by a source to be aware of a wealthy handsome chocolate man, she forgot to tell me he was funny and charming." Naomi

"I wish that source would have told you that I have discreetly already ordered the company's jet, and it will be in New Orleans within the 2 weeks…. Thought it may be a big surprise for my staff." Diamond responded.

"Oh you're so full of surprises, I can imagine," Naomi spoke in flirtation tone

Without any hesitation, Diamond leaned forward, and whispered to Naomi, "that depends on the situation, the moment and your experience…. while I define what is your standard, and how fast can I prodigiously exceed it."

Naomi smiled while the intercom announced that the plane boarding to Malta will begin in 15 minutes.

"So Mr. Asanti, will you be investing in a hotel or hotels while you are visiting Malta?" Naomi asked.

Diamond cracked a smile, and responded "That depends on the loose change I get back from the primary buy…. I think t will be smart if we make this look professional, so, you may leave first and I will see you, probably, in Malta, Ms. Naomi."

"Diamond, darling, not if I see you first," Naomi spoke as she grabbed her purse and walked to the boarding gate to board the plane. Diamond watched her as she strolled away, admiring her toned curves.

Twenty-seven minutes away from landing, Kendra tapped Diamond on the shoulder while he was napping and said, "Mr. Diamond, Mr. Diamond, we're less than 30 minutes away from landing."

Diamond yearns and stretch in his chair, and turn around to his staff who were up and ready to give their undivided attention with notepads in one hand and a pen in the other.

"Ok team, quick walkthrough, you all know the drill, Ms. Well how is the itinerary looking?" Diamond asked Kendra

"Yes Mr. Diamond, we have the transportation waiting at the airport, with your rental and our rooms are ready when we arrive. We will be using the International Investment Group (IIG) Bank, located in Sliema. Once we all get settled in the hotel, we will go to the bank to get our cards for per diem, I have scheduled for our transportation to leave our hotel at

2:30. The meeting has been moved up to tomorrow with the Hawkin, Jesus, and Company for 12 pm, so rest up. And we will have an extra night in Malta." Kendra announced

"Thank you, Ms. Well, Mr. Barker, what percentage of equity are we leaving with?" Diamond asked KyDouglas

"Mr. Diamond, I have reviewed the numbers, and received consultation from Mr. Downing, we can leave with less than 30% but no lower than 20%. If we reach below 25%, then we will buy the abandon open auditorium, an entertainment venue, less than 1 block away from the hotel. I had the privilege of speaking with Ms. Amy Cutajar, Senior Associate of Sliema Property and Estate Agency. There are a lot of bidders for the auditorium, but ready cash is ready for the opportunity." KyDouglas responded

Diamond went backed to Kendra with more questions, "Ms. Kendra, how many shares of Eurobonds did Raymond purchased for our approved MIIP. And do you have the report for this auditorium?"

"Over 500 thousand shares of Eurobonds, sir. The auditorium will need some renovation, but it is manageable and well below our budget." Kendra responded

"How much did we budget?" Diamond asked Kendra

"A little bit over 42 million pounds, sir!" Kendra responded

"Thank you, Kendra!" Diamond

"You're welcome Mr. Asanti." Kendra

"Ok, let's hit the ground running. Mr. Barker, call Ms. Cutajar when you get to the hotel, and tell her to have the paperwork ready." Diamond

"Yes, sir!" KyDouglas responded with excitement.

"Ms. Ida, you, me and KyDouglas going to take a look at the auditorium today when you all come back from the bank. If things are manageable, we take it tonight." Diamond

"Yes, Mr. Asanti!" Ida

"Please fasten your seatbelts and place your seat upright. We will be landing in 10 minutes." Announced by the flight attendant over the intercom.

Diamond and his team arrived at the airport and then separated as Diamond gets in his convertible rental and the team ride in the stretched sports utility vehicle.

"See you at the hotel and be ready," Diamond yelled as he drove off with the top down.

Instead of going straight to the spa resort as mapquest routed, Diamond decided to make up his own scenic route as he navigated from Triq Marina to Tigne Seafront. The time Diamond arrived, the team have already left to go to the bank. Arriving at the resort, Diamond received his key card from the front desk and went to his suite.

With the view of overlooking the Mediterranean sea to the Manoel Island, Diamond deeply inhale and exhale as he comes to the realization that he is living his purpose.

Naomi arrived at her cousin's office, Ms. Amy Cutajar, to say hello, and catch up on Malta's business affairs. Speaking in their Maltese language, Amy let Naomi know that she is meeting with a potential buyer within the hour.

Naomi asked, "An American named Diamond Asanti?

Amy replied "No, his name is KyDouglas Barker of Shupavu Equity. He sounded very handsome."

Naomi responded "Yes, yes, that is Diamond Asanti's company. The man is a billionaire but doesn't own a jet."

Amy asked, "How do you know of this man? Is he buying Hotel Gortina?"

Naomi answered, "I don't know if he is buying it all up, or an equity amount. What is he coming to see you for?"

Amy responded, "His company interest in the Pietru Awditorju."

Naomi responded, "The pietru awditorju has been closed for 3 years, why would he want that place?"

Meanwhile, Diamond and his team completed a quick assessment of the auditorium and amenities before traveling to Amy's office. As they arrive, Naomi and Amy were finishing up their conversation about Malta's business affairs and their interesting guests.

Diamond opened the front door to let Ida and KyDouglas walk in first, as Naomi walked toward them.

Diamond than opened the front door to let Naomi out. "Such a gentleman, Mr. Asanti," Naomi spoke as she walked pass Diamond

Diamond did not respond, he just grinned, watching Naomi walk to her car.

"Good afternoon Ms. Cutajar, I am KyDouglas Barker of Shupavu Equity, great to finally meet you…." KyDouglas

"Likewise" Amy

"….. this is my colleague, Ms. Ida Walker….." KyDouglas

"Hello" Ida

"Good afternoon, as you would say in America" Amy

"….. and this individual is the owner of Shupavu Equity, Mr. Diamond Asanti." KyDouglas

"Good afternoon Ms. Cutajar, thank you for fitting us n your schedule." Diamond

"Of course Mr. Asanti, your associate Mr. Barker seemed very umh, passionate about the property I am going to show you. " Amy

Diamond gave KyDouglas a pat on the shoulder and said, "Yes, my team see the company's vision and develop a passion to attain and obtain it. Victory!... It's a wonderful feeling."

Everyone smiled and then Ida begins her new pitch followed by the use of Diamond's word "Victory" as all eyes locked on her, "Victory is a wonderful term we use at Shupavu Equity, hear it once, and it's perfect. No second thoughts, every transaction set in front of us are to either be delivered or be tasked in exceeding client's standards and watch it manifest as our business help them reach their vision. In so many other terms Ms. Cutajar, we are in the business of not only accomplishing but flourishing at an achievement so high, that our company does not ask for attention, attention finds us. And since attention finds us, we want it to find Malta. With that, we want them to ask, why is Shupavu so internationally exotic or the fact that we can find them with their first international transaction being with Sliema Property & Estate Agency. This is an opportunity for indirect advertisement Ms. Cutajar of not being just an agency, but a client."

KyDouglas then gave his pitch paraphrasing parts of Pietru Caxaro's Cantilena poem in English while Amy was tuned into the thoughts of what Ida had pitched.

> "It fell, my building, its foundations collapsed;
>
> It was not the builders' fault, but the rock gave away,
>
> Where I had hoped to find a rock, I found loose clay
>
> It feels, my edifice, which I had been building for so long,
>
> And so, my edifice subsided, AND I SHALL HAVE TO BUILD IT UP AGAIN"

"The Pietru Auditorium is a unique dedication to the late philosopher Mr. Pietru Caxaro, however, it has been abandon for more than 2 years…." KyDouglas

"Mr. Barker, how did you know it has been closed for more than 2 years?" Amy asked

"We do our research, Ms. Amy. Historically speaking, a lot of vacant buildings here in Malta has a story of being abandoned, forgotten or sold to be a club with extreme depreciation. We don't want that for this prestige edifice...... So your listing price is 1.4 million pounds, looking at the renovations and other upgrades, we are offering to buy the property at 1.25 million pounds today! And best believe this is just the beginning." KyDouglas spoke

Amy then looked at Diamond who was staring at the window admiring the sea overview.

"Are you willing to buy it now Mr. Asanti?" Amy asked as she turned her attention to him.

Diamond then turned around and requested for Ms. Walker to present the blank check.

"We did not travel this far to leave empty handed Ms. Cutajar. We're willing and ready to sign the check if you are ready to make the transaction." Diamond spoke as he makes direct eye contact with Amy.

Amy smiled and said, "I take it there is no need to drive over to the auditorium then, I'll go and get the paperwork."

After completing the transaction, that evening Diamond and his team met at the bar of the hotel to celebrate.

"One down, one to go. Here is to a great team and a great company. Way to hit the ground running Y'all. Cin cin." Diamond making a toast amongst his staff.

Ida then spotted Naomi walking in and acknowledge Diamond, "Your mystery friend is here."

Diamond turned around to take a look and then looked back at his staff, "Everybody, enjoy yourselves, gets some rest... We have a big deal to take care of tomorrow."

Diamond then left the table and walked toward Naomi while her back was turned, seated at the bar.

"There he goes.... Businessman during the day, flirter at night." Ida said

"That's the beauty of being wealthy, and single, speaking of which, let's go out," Kendra responded

 "Let's do it!" KyDouglas

"She will have a raspberry martini and I hope you have Grey Goose Vodka." Diamond tells the bartender as he walks up on Naomi. "Ms. Naomi, nice to see you again. Are you staying here?"

Both then making direct eye contact.

Naomi in her red coral matelassé silk dress, "Diamond, congratulation on the Pietru purchase.... I wonder what are your intentions?"

"News travels fast around here I see," Diamond responded

"Darling, a dashing wealthy American man does not fly over 5,000 miles just to buy an auditorium. What else is in your mysterious bag of acquisition Mr. Asanti? You're shopping, but not on impulse. You want this.... hotel as well? You have a very discreet plan?" Naomi

"Naomi, DARLING, discretion with diversity is the beauty of a holding company. Not greed, but to acquire a fair share of ownership when you are in a position like I am." Diamond

"No, it's the beauty of the business and capitalism....." Naomi

"Tomato, toomaytoe, laissez-faire.... Are you staying in Gortini as well?" Diamond quick response with a smile.

"No, I have a villa on the outside here in Sliema." Naomi

"Nice.... Since I am in the mood of buying, would you like to sale it? I can use a vacation villa." Diamond

"Is this impulse talking you are doing handsome?" Naomi

Diamond smiled and leaned as if he was reacting the same he was in the London's airport, "maybe, but... that depends on the situation, the moment and your experience."

"My experience is telling me to say thank you for the drink Diamond. I shall see you tomorrow and your French is horrible. Goodnight dear." Naomi

Naomi gives Diamond a kiss on the cheek as she begins to get up, Diamond spoke, "Well this was absolutely a short conversation, but tomorrow could be a long day."

The next day in the meeting between Diamond's team and the HJC's negotiation team of which includes Naomi Ripard, the Director of Contracting and Purchasing, a series of conclusionary offers and counter-offers were administered as if it was a game of ping pong. Diamond did not say anything as of yet aside from the greeting, as Kendra plays quarterback, handing the ball off to Ida, KyDouglas, and the retained lawyer to speak for Shupavu Equity.

"Ms. Walker, why you and your company feel that a 26.4 million pounds can get you 27% of our company?" Executive Team Member of HJC

Ida responded with such enthusiasm, "After researching, Shupavu sees that HJC is consistent with maintaining and expanding their brand in premier locations across Europe, and working on luxury commercial properties in Dubai. Yet, Hotel Gortina has been open for less than 10 years, and only have an annual average shy of 1.4% gross profit."

KyDouglas quickly harmonized in on Ida's intro-pitch, and said, "We see no reason why Malta and Hotel Gortina cannot be better. As Ms. Ida stated, after doing our research, we have found the crumbs that can easily break a Torta tal-Marmurat. This spa resort is well kept, but when we look at the balance sheet between the Accounts Receivable and Accounts Payable, we see the opportunity for us to increase revenues while minimizing a spike on expenses. Our intentions are to add value and increase the profit margin along with taking the risk on our side."

Ida chimed in, "We will use our resources to bring attractions, entertainment, and people to Malta. Starting less than a block away from here. With this deal, we are bringing a new, colorful civilized beginning to Hotel Gortina and the community of Sliema, Malta with high net worth tourists. In return, this brings longevity to Malta and to this segment of Hawkins, Jesus, and Company. Our research has also shown that there are very few pounds spent on media to sponsor or in fact, advertisements for exposure to this resort….."

"We have become aware of your acquisition with the Pietru Auditorium. You say entertainment and attraction, understand Malta is a quiet island until sailors pull in port. What type of entertainment are you referring too?" Naomi asked

"Jazz Music, a genre appreciated all around the world. Coming from the heart of the Treme's New Orleans, Louisiana where it was born, and making a footprint here in Malta, year around. Starting down the street at the Pietru Awditorju. Let's think about it, the foot traffic, and we are attracting a genre fan base of wealthy sophisticated tourists not only from Africa and Europe but from the Middle East and Asia, all leading back to the Spa Resort, Hotel Gortina." KyDouglas

Finally, Diamond joined the cryptographic pitches between Ida and KyDouglas and went straight to the numbers with locked in eye contact.

"Everyone, the main focus of this all is money, and who is taking the risk. We all know for a fact that this percentage of equity in Hotel Gortina is all down to the number, but we're looking at reality. As Mr. KyDouglas stated, we are taking on the risk. Hawkin, Jesus & Company has really moved on from

Malta, and the percentage we are asking for is no more higher than what your government receives just to govern, which means doing nothing in most parts of your business. With our deal, you will still have majority shares and with less risk. My final offer for 27% equity, is 26.8 million pounds." Diamond spoke with a stern look.

Diamond and his team have convinced the board that they know more than the representatives of HJC know about their own business and sold on them on the marketing strategy and the new thought of making the company profitable. Shupavu now owns 27% equity of Hotel Gortina Spa Resort and 100% equity of Pietru Awditorju.

"Shupavu Team, congratulations on more profitable responsibilities." Diamond as he raised his glass on a successful acquisition.

"Cheer Cheers" all spoke as a team.

Diamond takes his last sip of his drink, and place his glass down, and Naomi snuck up behind him, "He will have another Courvoisier Cognac and I'll have a raspberry martini."

 "The Lovely Naomi, how are you darling?" Diamond with a handsome grin on his face as he looks Naomi directly in her eyes.

"Congratulation on your accomplishments, I see you are celebrating." Naomi

"Honey, every day is a celebration." Diamond

"Elaborate my dear." Naomi

"Because personally, I wake up and get to do what I want to do, and become profitably successful in doing it. It's the life!" Diamond

"I bet that is truly a fascinating lifestyle? Always staying on top." Naomi

The eye contact between Naomi and Diamond begins to intensify in a softcore flirting type of manner. They both smile as if they are reading each other mind and agrees on the intention of what is to be left in store for the rest of the evening.

Diamond than leaned forward, and whispered, "I am not selfish, I enjoy being on top, but I also enjoy imagining you, I mean….. watching others enjoy being on top as well. It's an incredible feeling that should be shared."

Naomi looked at Diamond with an enduring look and responded "Diamond, Iahgalwantta havfunbeinnatughty tonight. Can you help me close the deal on that tonight?"

"Of course I can, I am a great team player…. Is it okay if I can see the countryside Sliema, meaning your villa?" Diamond spoke with a smirk as if he was prepared for rejection.

Naomi responded, "No my dear, I am going to have a couple more drinks and shag you tonight in your new hotel."

Diamond then smiled because to him it is the Diamond life.

……. Bringing Jazz To Malta, Hotel Gortina…….

www.ingramcontent.com/pod-product-compliance
Lightning Source LLC
Chambersburg PA
CBHW030136260626
47156CB00008B/2971